VOLCA WOMAN

Rosalind Kerven

Illustrated by Chris Molan

CAMBRIDGE
UNIVERSITY PRESS

It was the happiest time of year on the Big Island
of Hawaii. The Festival was starting!

The air was full of tasty smells: roast pig, roast chicken
and baked fish. There was drumming, singing and dancing,
and lots of people were surfing on the blue waves.

It was the best party ever.

Ah . . . but soon something terrible,
really terrible, was going to happen!

Someone shouted, "Stand back! It's time for the chiefs to have their race!"

The chiefs strode out of the crowd. They were all huge, strong men. Each one was pulling a sledge. They marched to the top of a grassy hill and waited there in a line.

"Get ready . . . GO!"

The chiefs rushed forward. They threw themselves onto their sledges . . .

           then down,

                down,

                   down

they came, faster and faster to the bottom . . .

"Chief Kaha-wali is the winner!"

The whole crowd clapped and cheered.
What a noise they made!

There was a mountain near the Festival place. A strange old woman lived deep inside it. At that moment she lay fast asleep.

In her sleep she heard the clapping and cheering. It woke her up. Oh-ho, she was angry!

She jumped out of her mountain and ran down to
see what was going on.

"Be quiet!" she screeched. "How dare you make
so much noise?"

"I am very sorry," said Chief Kaha-wali. "They are cheering me because I am the champion. I have just won the sledge race."

The old woman snorted.

"Pah!" she cried. "What nonsense! Do you really think there is something special about you, young man? Just you try racing on your sledge against *me*. You will see, I can easily beat you, Kaha-wali. Then *I* shall be the champion!"

Now Kaha-wali was angry.

"Never!" he said. "How can I race against a woman? Sledging is only for men."

"Do as I say," hissed the old woman. "If you don't, you will be very sorry."

She shook her finger fiercely and glared at him with
her deep, black eyes. Then Kaha-wali felt afraid. Maybe
she could work bad magic?

"All right," he agreed at last, "I shall race against you."

They walked up the hill together, the strong chief
and the weak, old woman.
"Get ready . . . GO!"
They each zoomed down on a sledge.

Kaha-wali won easily again.

"You cheated!" the old woman screamed at him.
"You only won because you had a better sledge
than mine. Swap your sledge with mine
– and then let us race again."

"No," replied Kaha-wali.
"Go away, you silly old woman!"

He turned his back on her and
walked off.

"Don't you be rude to me!" the old woman cried. Then suddenly she began to change. First, her eyes glowed, red and orange. Then her hair crackled and burst into hot flames!

The old woman stamped her foot: STAMP, STAMP, STAMP!

The ground shook. The houses shook and fell to pieces. The trees shook and tumbled down. The whole island shook . . .

Yes, that old woman, she made an *earthquake*!

The old woman turned round and called out to her mountain, "BURN!"

At once the top of the mountain cracked open. Great lumps of rock jumped out of it in a blaze of red-hot fire. They melted in the heat and went rushing and gushing down the mountain-side.

Kaha-wali stood there, watching her. "I can see that you are very powerful," he said softly. "So tell me, madam, who are you?"

The old woman did not answer at first, for she
was changing again.

Her wrinkles disappeared and her face became
beautiful. Her bent old body grew straight
and strong and young. She spread
out her arms and shouted,

"I am Pele! I am the great Lady of Fire! This burning mountain is my own volcano. You have dared to laugh at me, Kaha-wali. I shall use my fire to punish you!"

Pele was like a hot wind. She ran up to the top of her volcano. She roared like thunder. Lightning sparkled from her fingertips. Her whole body seemed to turn into dancing, yellow flames.

Then down she came again – *WHOOSH!* – down the mountain-side, pushing a river of lava and burning rock before her. "Kaha-wali," she shrieked, "I'M COMING TO GET YOU!"

Everyone ran! Kaha-wali and the other chiefs, the drummers and dancers, the surfers and singers, all of them ran away in terror.

But the goddess ignored them all except for Kaha-wali.

"Come back here, you coward!" she called after him. "What? Is a great chief like you really afraid of me? Stop, I tell you, stop and take your punishment!"

Kaha-wali raced on and on. He could feel Pele's hot breath on him, getting closer and closer behind. He ran past his dear old mother, his sweet wife and his two young children, and shouted a sad "Goodbye!" to them all.

He did not stop until he came to a beach. There was a boat there. Kaha-wali pushed it down to the water. Then he jumped inside and sailed away.

The sea was cool and wet. Surely he was safe here?

Yes, he was safe.

Pele came burning after him, right down to the shore.
But then . . . she had to stop. For water is stronger than
fire. Pele knew that if she went into the sea, her fire
would go out and she would die.

Now her anger turned back like the tide, and grew cold.
She shook herself and sighed.

Then she walked slowly away, back to the deep darkness of her mountain.

Kaha-wali sailed far away over
the sea, until he came to another island.
He lived there quietly for the rest of his
days, safe from Pele's anger.

That great chief died long, long ago.
But the people of Hawaii say that Pele is
still alive, for every so often her volcano
still bursts into flames.

Perhaps, one day, you might go there and see it for yourself . . . But if you do, be careful. Don't do anything to make Pele cross, or she might send her fire after *you*!

About the people who told this story

This story was first told hundreds of years ago by the Polynesian people who lived in Hawaii. Hawaii is a group of tropical islands in the middle of the Pacific Ocean.

The old Hawaiian people were great sailors and explorers. They were very clever at making wooden boats, and they used bark-cloth and feathers to make beautifully decorated clothes.

Today Hawaii is part of the United States of America.